Explorers of North America

CHRISTINE TAYLOR-BUTLER

Children's Press®
An Imprint of Scholastic Inc.
New York Toronto London Auckland Sydney
Mexico City New Delhi Hong Kong
Danbury, Connecticut

Content Consultant

David R. Smith, PhD

Academic Adviser and Adjunct Assistant Professor of History

University of Michigan–Ann Arbor

Reading Consultant

Cecilia Minden-Cupp, PhD

Early Literacy Author and Consultant

Library of Congress Cataloging-in-Publication Data

Taylor-Butler, Christine.
 Explorers of North America / by Christine Taylor-Butler.
    p. cm.—(A true book)
 Includes bibliographical references and index.
 Audience: Grades 4–6.
 ISBN-13: 978-0-531-12632-5 (lib. bdg.)   978-0-531-14782-5 (pbk.)
 ISBN-10: 0-531-12632-3 (lib. bdg.)   0-531-14782-7 (pbk.)
 1. America—Discovery and exploration—European—Juvenile literature. 2. America—Discovery
and exploration—Juvenile literature. 3. Explorers—America—Biography—Juvenile literature.
4. Explorers—North America—Biography—Juvenile literature. 5. Explorers—Europe—
Biography—Juvenile literature. I. Title.
 E121.T39 2008
 970.01—dc22   2007012255

Find the Truth!

Everything you are about to read is true *except* for one of the sentences on this page.

Which one is **TRUE**?

T or F   Christopher Columbus was the first European to set foot on North America.

T or F   Spanish explorers searched for a city of gold.

Find the answer in this book. →

Short School
Library Book

Contents

1 Europeans Explore the Americas

Who really made it here first? 7

2 A Trade Route to Asia

What were all these explorers looking for? . . . 10

3 The Search for Gold

Did any explorers actually find a city of gold? 17

4 In Search of the Northwest Passage

Was that sea route ever found? 23

Christopher Columbus

Lewis and Clark's compass

THE BIG TRUTH!

Packing for the Unknown

What do you bring if you don't know
where you're going? 30

5 The Corps of Discovery

What was on the land we bought? 32

6 Modern Explorers

What's left to explore today? 39

True Statistics 43
Resources 44
Important Words......... 46
Index 47
About the Author 48

Lewis and Clark encountered almost 50 different Native American groups on their journey west to the Pacific Ocean.

This painting shows Christopher Columbus leaving Palos, Spain, in 1492. Columbus sailed across the Atlantic hoping to find a trade route to Asia. His three ships were called the *Niña*, the *Pinta*, and the *Santa Maria*.

CHAPTER 1

Europeans Explore the Americas

It took Columbus 70 days to cross about 4,000 miles of the Atlantic Ocean.

Christopher Columbus

Every October, Americans gather for parades to honor one of the world's most famous explorers. His name is Christopher Columbus. Some people think Columbus was the first European explorer to reach the Americas. But another explorer beat him by about 500 years.

The Vikings Are Here!

Leif Erikson was born in Iceland in the year 970. His family later moved to Greenland. There he heard stories about unexplored lands to the west.

Erikson was a **Viking**. The Vikings were people from northern Europe who were famous for their sailing skills.

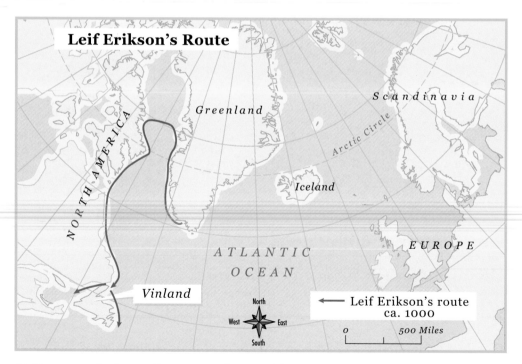

Erikson took the safest route he could. He stuck to the coast and then crossed the ocean at its narrowest point.

This illustration shows Leif Erikson on his voyage to Canada. He took with him a crew of 34 Viking men.

Erikson set sail in search of new lands to explore. He landed on the coast of what is now Canada in about the year 1000. Erikson named the area Vinland. He built a **settlement** there.

The settlement lasted only a few years. Native Americans had long lived in the area. The Vikings may have left after fighting with the Native Americans.

CHAPTER 2

A Trade Route to Asia

Traders used camels and other animals to carry goods from Asia to the Mediterranean Sea.

In the 1400s, many European traders traveled to China and India. The Europeans bought silk and spices in Asia. They brought these goods back to Europe to sell.

These are the ruins of a city in China that was along the Silk Road, or the trade route between Europe and China.

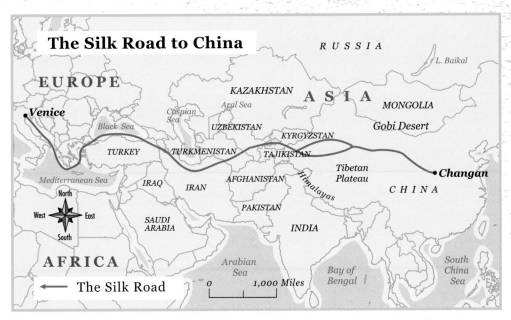

The trade route to China was called the Silk Road. Traders faced many dangers, such as blazing-hot deserts, bandits, and wars.

European traders had to travel over land to reach Asia. The trip was thousands of miles long and could take years. They had to cross mountains and deserts. The traders wanted to find a sea route to China. This would make the journey much faster and less expensive. The explorer who discovered this route would become famous and wealthy.

We've Found Asia! Or Have We?

China lies to the east of Europe. So most European explorers looked east for a sea route. An Italian explorer named Christopher Columbus had a different idea. He wanted to sail west to reach Asia. Many people thought he was crazy!

Sailing trips were expensive. Columbus needed to find someone to pay for his trip. King Ferdinand II and Queen Isabella of Spain agreed to give Columbus money. They also gave him three ships: the *Niña*, the *Pinta*, and the *Santa Maria*.

Here, King Ferdinand II and Queen Isabella promise Columbus money for his voyage.

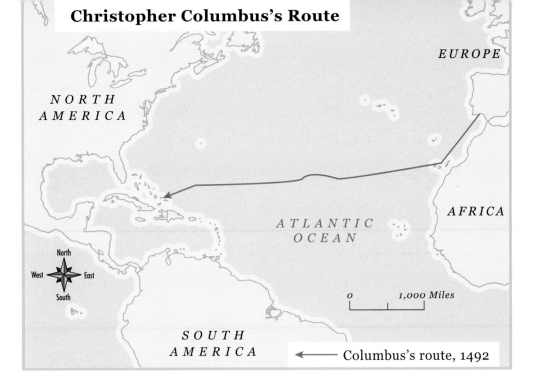

Christopher Columbus's Route

EUROPE

NORTH
AMERICA

AFRICA

ATLANTIC
OCEAN

North

West   East

South

0   1,000 Miles

SOUTH
AMERICA

⟵ Columbus's route, 1492

On August 3, 1492, Columbus and his crew set sail. On October 12, they reached land. Columbus thought he had reached Asia. He sailed back to Spain with the good news.

Of course, Columbus did not really sail to Asia. What he found was an island in what is now the Bahamas. The Bahamas is a group of islands near North America. The islands were part of what Europeans began to call "the New World."

Trying to Get to Asia . . . Again!

John Cabot also tried to sail west to find a route to Asia. He thought he could find a shorter route if he headed further to the north than other explorers.

Cabot set sail from England in 1497. Like Columbus, he reached land he believed was in Asia. It was really Newfoundland, which is now part of Canada. Cabot and his crew began a second journey in 1498. They were never heard from again.

Exploring was dangerous. Storms sank ships. Ships got lost because of **navigation** errors. Sailors ran out of supplies and starved. What happened to Cabot and his crew? No one knows.

In 1997, this replica of John Cabot's ship sailed to Newfoundland, 500 years after the original voyage.

What Is in a Name?

Columbus thought he had sailed to Asia. Who figured out he was wrong? It was an Italian explorer named Amerigo Vespucci (am-ahr-IH-go ves-PYOO-chee). Vespucci explored the southwest coast of South America in 1501. The land was bigger than anyone had thought.

Vespucci was convinced that the land was not Asia. Instead, it was a "new world." A German mapmaker read about Vespucci's discovery. He made

a map of the new lands. He called it America, in Vespucci's honor. Obviously, the name stuck!

Before he became an explorer, Amerigo Vespucci liked to collect maps.

These are ruins of the Aztec emperor Montezuma's summer palace outside of Mexico City, Mexico. Montezuma died in a battle against Spanish invaders in 1520.

CHAPTER 3

The Search for Gold

Mexico City is built on the ruins of the Aztec capital.

By the 1500s, people in Spain were hearing tales of an amazing city in the Americas. The city's buildings were made of gold. Some called it El Dorado (EL doh-RAH-doh), "the city of gold." Spanish explorers wanted to find this **mythical** city.

Defeating the Aztecs

In 1518, Spanish explorer Hernán Cortés (ehr-NAHN kor-TESS) set sail with 11 ships. He was determined to find gold. He arrived at the land now called Mexico. The local people told Cortés about the Aztecs. They told him the Aztecs had great riches.

Cortés led his men into the Aztec capital. It was larger than any European city at the time. The Aztec leader, Montezuma, welcomed Cortés. He gave Cortés gifts of gold and let him stay in his palace.

The Aztec people treated Cortés warmly. According to some sources, they believed he was a human form of their god Quetzalcoatl (KET-suhl-kuh-WAH-tuhl).

It took more than two years for Cortés and his men to defeat the Aztecs.

Montezuma greeted Cortés formally in 1519. Soon Cortés made the ruler a prisoner in his own palace.

But Cortés wanted the Aztecs' wealth. He took Montezuma prisoner. His troops fought the Aztecs and won. Cortés claimed the Aztec land for Spain. He sent back ships loaded with Aztec treasures. Spain declared him a hero.

Cortés's victory gave Spain land in the New World. The land became a Spanish **colony** called New Spain.

The Lost City of Gold

Francisco Coronado was governor of part of New Spain. He sent men into the wilderness in search of a city of gold. One man claimed to have found it.

Coronado set out in search of this city in 1540. He traveled north for more than four months. Finally, he reached what is now New Mexico. There he found the Zuni (ZOO-nee) people. They did not live in a golden city. They lived in buildings made from a mixture of mud and straw. Coronado was angry. He wanted gold but found only mud! Coronado threatened to make the Zuni slaves. So the Zuni attacked him.

Coronado's men defeated the Zuni. But they never found their golden city.

There were no horses in the Americas before the Spanish brought them there.

Coronado's exploration of what is now the southwestern United States lasted for about two years. Coronado took more than 1,600 men with him on the journey.

This ship was built to look like the *Half Moon*, the ship that Henry Hudson sailed up the Hudson River. In 2002, it sailed from New York City to Albany, New York.

CHAPTER 4

In Search of the Northwest Passage

While looking for the Northwest Passage, English explorer Henry Hudson nearly reached the North Pole!

Europeans still wanted to find a way to reach Asia by traveling west. Some explorers searched North America for a water route connecting the Atlantic and Pacific oceans. They called this route the **Northwest Passage**.

Henry Hudson

Finding Fool's Gold

Jacques Cartier (zhahk kar-tyay) sailed west from France in 1534. He arrived at the mouth of the St. Lawrence River in what is now Canada.

There Cartier met the Iroquois. They told him tales of a wealthy kingdom. Cartier's men searched for it. They found what they thought were gold and diamonds. They were wrong. Their gold was a shiny **mineral** called fool's gold. Their diamonds were made from a sparkly mineral called quartz.

This painting shows Jacques Cartier and his men at the mouth of the St. Lawrence River. They came across many native people on their journey.

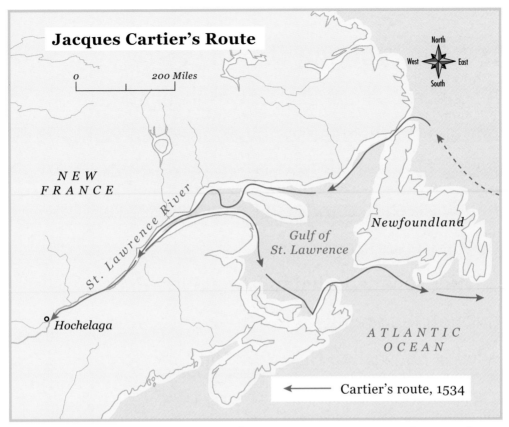

Jacques Cartier's Route

0   200 Miles

North
West — East
South

NEW
FRANCE

St. Lawrence River

Gulf of
St. Lawrence

Newfoundland

Hochelaga

ATLANTIC
OCEAN

⟵ Cartier's route, 1534

At 1,900 miles (3,058 kilometers) long, the St. Lawrence is one of the world's 25 longest rivers. It does not reach the Pacific Ocean, as Cartier had hoped.

Cartier followed the St. Lawrence River. He was hoping the river would bring him to the Pacific Ocean. It did not. But Cartier saw many animals along the river. Later, French fur traders would come to trap some of these animals.

Rebellion on the *Discovery*

An Englishman named Henry Hudson tried to find the Northwest Passage in 1609. Hudson sailed far, far to the north. He was so far north that he nearly reached the North Pole. He was stopped by the ice and cold.

Hudson then tried to find a route to Asia through the middle of North America. He found what is now called New York Harbor.

In 1609, Henry Hudson searched for a water route across North America. Here, Native Americans near the mouth of the Hudson River go forward in canoes to welcome him.

Hudson's son John was only a teenager when he was cast adrift at sea. Father and son were lost forever.

Hudson thought he had finally found his passage. He sailed up the river that now bears his name—the Hudson River. He sailed as far as Albany, New York. He was forced to turn back because the river became too narrow for his ship. One year later, Hudson tried again. His ship, the *Discovery*, reached Hudson Bay in Canada. The ship became trapped by ice. He and his sailors camped for months in the cold. In the spring, his crew wanted to go home. Hudson refused. So the crew rebelled. They put Hudson, his son, and seven others in a boat.

They gave them no food or water. Then they set them adrift. Hudson was never seen again.

Cook Tries Another Route

James Cook served in the British navy. From 1768 to 1771, he explored the South Pacific. He and his men were the first Europeans to find Australia.

But the British were still eager to find a new route to Asia. The government offered a huge cash prize to any explorer who could find the Northwest Passage. In 1776, Cook gave it a try.

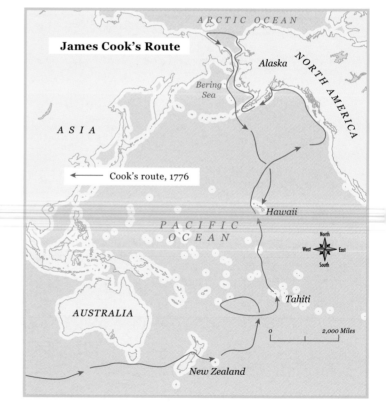

James Cook's last exploration took him to many places. Starting from England, he and his crew sailed to New Zealand, Tahiti, Hawaii, and Alaska.

The Panama Canal allows ships to travel between the Pacific Ocean and the Caribbean Sea. It took ten years to build the canal, which is 48 miles (77 km) long.

He sailed south from England around Africa, then headed east toward North America. Cook sailed up the west coast, searching for the passage. He didn't find it. On the way back home, he stopped in Hawaii. There, Cook was killed fighting with native peoples.

Explorers never found a way to sail across the Americas. So people built one in Central America. It's called the Panama Canal! It opened in 1914.

A Traveling Library

a dictionary

at least two books about classifying plants

at least two books about astronomy

a map of the Missouri River

Giving someone a peace medal meant that you did not have violent intentions.

Presents for Native Americans

144 small mirrors

4,600 sewing needles

144 small scissors

Jefferson peace medals

8 brass kettles

10 pounds (5kg) of thread

silk ribbons

33 pounds (15 kg) of tiny beads

Beads

Map of the Mississippi River

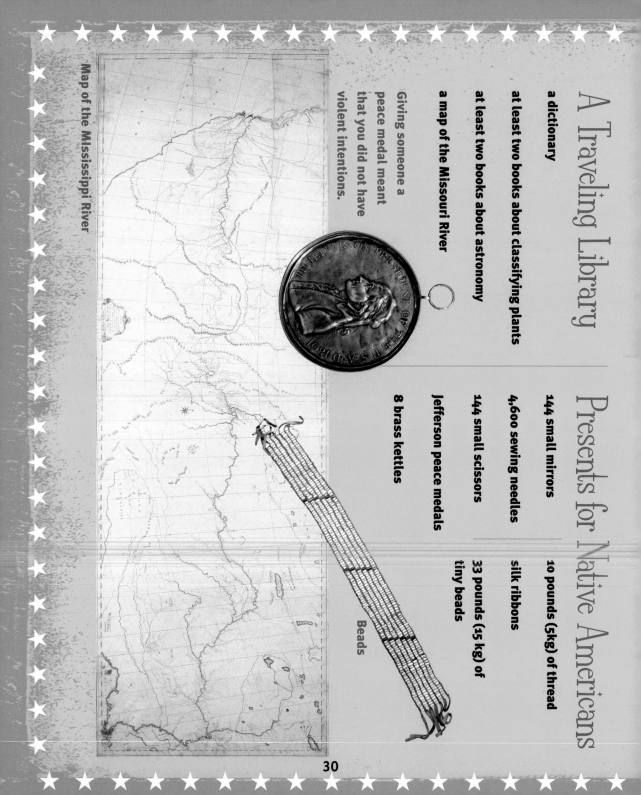

Packing for the Unknown

You're taking a two-year trip into the wilderness. What do you pack? Meriwether Lewis and William Clark were going to explore a new part of the United States. They had $2,500 to spend. Here are some of the things they bought:

Supplies

a telescope

compasses to tell them their direction

thermometers

150 yards (137 meters) of cloth to make tents and sheets (that's enough to cover one and a half football fields)

pliers, chisels, and handsaws

hatchets

15 rifles

420 pounds (191 kilograms) of steel to make bullets

176 pounds (80kg) of gunpowder

30 steels (pieces of metal used to start fires)

a corn mill to grind corn

24 tablespoons

shoes and socks

mosquito nets

10 pounds (5 kg) of fishing line and fishing hooks

12 pounds (5 kg) of soap

193 pounds (88 kg) of "portable soup," a paste made from beef, eggs, and vegetables

3 bushels (106 liters) of salt

paper, ink, and crayons

45 flannel shirts

woolen pants

CHAPTER 5

The Corps of Discovery

Lewis and Clark discovered 122 kinds of animals, including the grizzly bear.

Would you buy something without knowing what it was? That's what the United States did in 1803. President Thomas Jefferson paid France $15 million for 800,000 square miles (2 million sq km) of land. This land was west of the Mississippi River.

In this painting, Lewis and Clark encounter a group of Native Americans.

The Team of Lewis and Clark

The land that Jefferson bought in 1803 doubled the size of the United States. But nobody in the United States knew much about the land. Jefferson sent Meriwether Lewis and William Clark to explore it.

Lewis was Jefferson's personal secretary. He was also an explorer. Clark had served in the army with Lewis. Both men knew how to survive in the wilderness.

This drawing from Clark's journal introduced Americans to the white salmon trout, now known as the coho or silver salmon.

Jefferson told Lewis and Clark to travel west to the Pacific Ocean. They were sent to study the people, plants, land, and animals along the way. Jefferson wanted answers to many questions. Was there a river flowing west all the way to the Pacific? How high were the Rocky Mountains? Were the Native Americans friendly?

Lewis and Clark formed a group of almost 50 men called the "**Corps** of Discovery." On May 14, 1804, the corps left St. Louis, Missouri. They began a hard journey on the Missouri River. The men often had to paddle upstream. Sometimes they had to get out and pull their boats. They covered less than 14 miles (23 km) each day.

Clark was a terrible speller. In his journal, he spelled mosquito 15 different ways!

The men reached present-day North Dakota after several months. They camped there for the winter. Two people joined the group. One was a Native American woman named Sacagawea (sah-kah-jah-WEE-uh). The other was her French husband, Toussaint Charbonneau (too-SAHN shar-bone-OH). The two were hired as **interpreters**. Many different Native American groups lived in the West. Sacagawea and her husband could help speak to them. They also knew the land well so they could help to guide the explorers.

Lewis and Clark reported "infinite numbers" of prairie dogs on their travels. The prairie dog population has fallen nearly 98 percent since that time.

Reaching the Pacific

By the summer of 1805, the corps reached Sacagawea's home in present-day Montana. They crossed the Rocky Mountains on horseback. They made dugout canoes and continued along a new river. In November, they finally reached the Pacific Ocean. It was a thrilling moment.

Their journey was not over yet. They still had to travel home. That took them another year. The men made it back to St. Louis in September 1806.

In two years, the Corps of Discovery traveled more than 8,000 miles (12,875 km). They never found a river running all the way to the Pacific Ocean. But they learned valuable information about the plants, animals, people, and land in the new American territory.

The Corps of Discovery Route

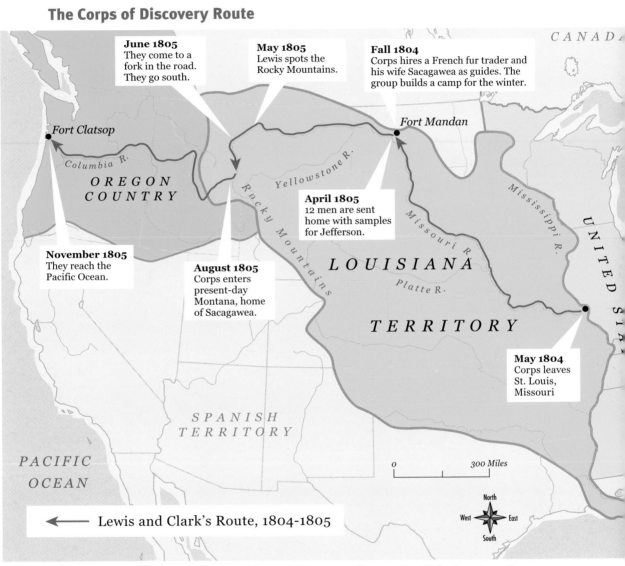

June 1805
They come to a fork in the road. They go south.

May 1805
Lewis spots the Rocky Mountains.

Fall 1804
Corps hires a French fur trader and his wife Sacagawea as guides. The group builds a camp for the winter.

Fort Mandan

April 1805
12 men are sent home with samples for Jefferson.

Fort Clatsop

Columbia R.

OREGON COUNTRY

Yellowstone R.

Rocky Mountains

Missouri R.

Mississippi R.

November 1805
They reach the Pacific Ocean.

August 1805
Corps enters present-day Montana, home of Sacagawea.

L O U I S I A N A

Platte R.

T E R R I T O R Y

UNITED STA[TES]

CANADA

May 1804
Corps leaves St. Louis, Missouri

SPANISH TERRITORY

PACIFIC OCEAN

0   300 Miles

North
West   East
South

⟵ Lewis and Clark's Route, 1804-1805

Exploring the Louisiana Purchase was a major task. This land makes up about 23 percent of the territory of the United States today!

Lewis and Clark ended their journey to the Pacific Ocean at present-day Cape Disappointment in Washington.

CHAPTER 6

Modern Explorers

Less than 5 percent of the ocean has been explored.

Lewis and Clark made their historic trip more than 200 years ago. Since then, people have continued to explore the world. Men and women have climbed tall mountains. They have cut their way through rain forests. Some explorers have even gone into space.

Lewis and Clark traveled within 50 miles (80 km) of what is now Glacier National Park in Montana.

39

Most of the explorers you've read about have been men. But there are many famous female explorers, too. In 1940, Barbara Wasburn climbed to the top of Alaska's Mount Bertha. She and her climbing partner, her husband, were the first people to ever climb the mountain. And in 1947, Barbara became the first woman to climb to the top of Mount McKinley, the tallest mountain in North America.

Barbara Washburn and her husband climbed Mount Bertha during their honeymoon.

Exploring Plants

One explorer risked her life to study plants. In 1927, Ynes Mexia (ee-NESS MEH-hyah) became a **botanist**, or plant scientist.

Mexia collected about 145,000 plant samples in her lifetime. She discovered as many as 500 new plant species. Mexia traveled in South America, Central America, and Alaska.

One time, she and her team were trapped at the bottom of a deep gorge in Peru for three months. Did Mexia panic? No! She was a true explorer. She spent the time searching the sides of the gorge for new plants!

Ynes Mexia started studying plants in college at the age of 51. She went on her first plant-collecting trip to Mexico at the age of 55.

New Discoveries

When you go exploring, you never know what you will find. Many explorers go looking for one thing. They find something completely different. Christopher Columbus was looking for a sea route. He found a **continent** instead.

Today's explorers search the oceans, outer space, and even parts of the human body. Explorers discover things that excite them. Their discoveries inspire other people to explore. That's what being an explorer is all about. ★

The Amazon rain forest remains largely unexplored. Thousands of animal and plant species are waiting to be discovered!

True Statistics

First European to find the Americas:
Leif Erikson, in about the year 1000

Explorer whom America is named after:
Amerigo Vespucci

Three explorers who searched for a city of gold:
Hernán Cortés, Francisco Coronado, and
Jacques Cartier

Cortés found: Aztec people and gold

Coronado found: Zuni people

Cartier found: Iroquois people, fool's gold,
and quartz

Distance Lewis and Clark traveled: 8,000 mi.
(12,875 km)

**Cost of supplies for Lewis and Clark's
two-year journey:** $2,500

Did you find the truth?

(F) Christopher Columbus was the first
European to set foot in North America.

(T) Spanish explorers searched for a
city of gold.

Resources

Books

Alter, Judy. *Extraordinary Explorers and Adventurers*. Danbury, CT: Children's Press, 2001.

Bergin, Mark. *You Wouldn't Want to Travel with Captain Cook! A Voyage You'd Rather Not Make*. Danbury, CT: Franklin Watts, 2006.

DeKeyser, Stacy. *Sacagawea*. Danbury, CT: Franklin Watts, 2004.

Macdonald, Fiona. *You Wouldn't Want to Sail with Christopher Columbus! Uncharted Waters You'd Rather Not Cross*. Danbury, CT: Franklin Watts, 2004.

Nardo, Don. *Francisco Coronado*. Danbury, CT: Franklin Watts, 2001.

Sansever-Dreher, Diane, and Ed Renfro. *Explorers Who Got Lost*. New York: Tor Books, 2005.

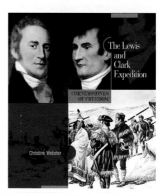

St. George, Judith. *So You Want to Be an Explorer*. New York: Philomel, 2005.

Webster, Christine. *The Lewis and Clark Expedition*. Danbury, CT: Children's Press, 2003.

Whitcraft, Melissa. *The Hudson River*. Danbury, CT: Franklin Watts, 2003.

Organizations and Web Sites

Hudson River Maritime Museum
www.hrmm.org
Find out more about Henry Hudson.

Lewis & Clark—The Journey of the Corps of Discovery
www.pbs.org/lewisandclark/index.html
Check out an interactive trail map of Lewis and Clark's route.

PBS: The Fall of the Aztecs
www.pbs.org/conquistadors/cortes/cortes_flat.html
Learn both sides of the story of the empire's conquest.

Places to Visit

Lewis and Clark National Historic Trail Interpretive Center
4201 Giant Springs Road
Great Falls, MT 59405-0900
406-727-8733
www.fs.fed.
us/r1/lewisclark/lcic/
Visit for programs about the Corps of Discovery.

The Mariners' Museum
100 Museum Drive
Newport News, VA 23606
757-591-7320
www.mariner.org/exhibitions/
Learn all about shipbuilding, navigation, and exploration.

Important Words

botanist – someone who studies plants

colony – lands settled and ruled by people from another country

continent – one of seven major bodies of land on Earth

corps (KOR) – a group of people acting or working together

interpreters – people who translate speech from one language to another

mineral – a substance in nature that isn't an animal or a plant

mythical (MITH-i-kuhl) – imaginary; existing in stories called myths or legends

navigation – the way of determining the position and course of ships at sea

Northwest Passage – a water route connecting the Atlantic and Pacific oceans, eventually discovered along the northern coast of North America

settlement – a place where a group of people live

Viking – one of a group of northern Europeans who explored the coasts of Europe and North America between the years 800 and 1100.

Index

Amazon rain forest, **42**
Aztec people, **16**, 17, **18–19**

Bahamas, 13
beads, **30**

Cabot, John, **14**
Cape Disappointment, **38**
Cartier, Jacques, **24**–25
Central America, 29, 41
Charbonneau, Toussaint, 35
Clark, William, 30–31, 32, **33**–35, 37, 38, 39
colonies, 19
Columbus, Christopher, **6**, **7**, **12**–13, 14, 15, 42
Cook, James, 28–29
Coronado, Francisco, 20, 21
Corps of Discovery, 34–35, 36, **37**
Cortés, Hernán, **18**, **19**

Discovery (ship), 27

El Dorado (City of Gold), 17, 20
Erikson, Leif, 8–**9**

Ferdinand II, king of Spain, **12**
fool's gold, 24
fur trade, 25, 37

Glacier National Park, **39**

Half Moon (ship), **22**
Hudson, Henry, **22**, **23**, **26**–27
Hudson, John, **27**
Hudson River, 27

Iroquois, **24**
Isabella, queen of Spain, **12**

Jefferson, Thomas, 32, 33, 34, 37

Lewis, Meriwether, 30–31, **33**–35, 37, 38, 39

maps, **8**, **11**, **13**, **25**, **28**, 30, **37**
Mexia, Ynes, **41**
Montezuma (Aztec leader), **16**, 18, **19**
Mount Bertha, **40**
Mount McKinley, 40

Native Americans, 9, **24**, **26**, 30, **33**, 34, 35
New Spain, 19
"New World," 13, 15, 19
New York Harbor, 26
Newfoundland, 14
Niña (ship), **6**, 12
North America, 13, 23, 26, 29, 40
Northwest Passage, 23, 26, 27, 28, 29

Panama Canal, **29**
peace medals, **30**
Pinta (ship), **6**, 12
prairie dogs, **35**

quartz, 24

Sacagawea, 35, 36, 37
Santa Maria (ship), **6**, 12
settlements, 9
Silk Road, **10**, **11**
South America, 15, 41
St. Lawrence River, **24**, **25**
storms, 14
supplies, 14, **30–31**

Vespucci, Amerigo, **15**
Vikings, 8–**9**

Washburn, Barbara, **40**
white salmon trout, **34**

Zuni people, 20

About the Author

Christine Taylor-Butler has written more than 30 books for children. She has written several books in the True Book American History series, including *The Bill of Rights*, *The Constitution*, *The Congress of the United States*, *The Supreme Court*, and *The Presidency*.

A native of Ohio, Taylor-Butler now lives in Kansas City, Missouri, with her husband, Ken, and their two daughters. She holds degrees in both civil engineering and art and design from the Massachusetts Institute of Technology.

PHOTOGRAPHS © 2008: AP Images: 3, 30 top right (Stepahnie S. Cordle), 14 (Keith Gosse), 22 (Mitch Jacobson); Courtesy of Bancroft Library, University of California, Berkeley: 41; Bridgeman Art Library International Ltd., London/New York: cover right (National Historical Park, Independence, Missouri, MO, U.S.A.), 30 bottom right (Peabody Essex Museum, Salem, MA); Corbis Images: back cover (Bettmann), 30 left (Robert Frazer), 35 (Joe McDonald), 39 (Neil Rabinowitz), 32 (Galen Rowell), 5, 31 top (Smithsonian Institution), 42 (Jim Zuckerman); Getty Images/C Squared Studios: 17; Landov, LLC/Thomas Winship/Boston Globe: 40; National Geographic Image Collection/Ira Block: 10, 43; Niebrugge Images/Ron Niebrugge: 38; PictureHistory.com: cover left; Scholastic Library Publishing, Inc.: 44; Superstock, Inc.: 4 top, 4 bottom, 6, 7, 33; The Art Archive/Picture Desk/Marc Charmet: 29; The Granger Collection, New York: 9, 12, 15, 18, 19, 21, 23, 24, 26, 31 bottom, 34; The Image Works: 27 (Mary Evans Picture Library), 16 (Werner Foreman/Topham).

MAPS by Bob Italiano